Spanish Roses

Other Books by
RONNIE SMITH

The Last White Ruby

The Royal Princess and the Three Magical Gifts

Roses for the Most High:
Poetry Celebrating the Mystical Christian Path

The Sky is for Wonder

Deployed Flight and Sometimes Eternity

Mystic lands and Celtic Saints

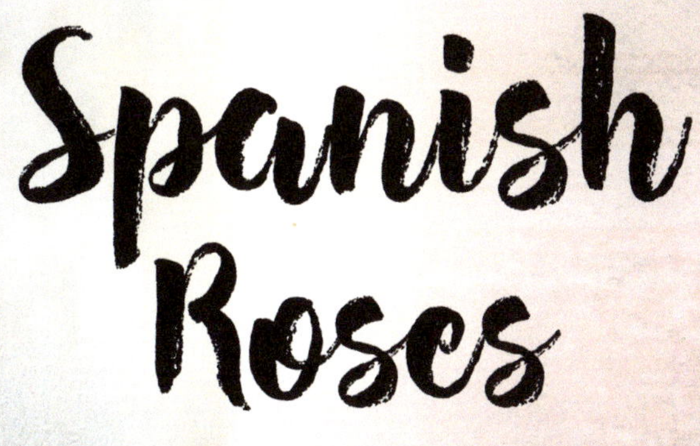

Spanish Roses

POETIC
REVELATION
OF THE
SPANISH
MYSTICS

RONNIE SMITH

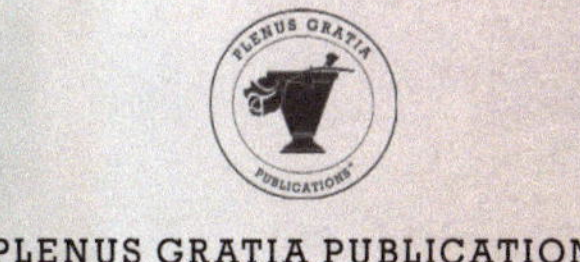

PLENUS GRATIA PUBLICATIONS

Ronnie Smith/Plenus Gratia Publications®
PlenusGratiaToday@gmail.com

Book Cover & Interior Design by The Book Cover Whisperer:
OpenBookDesign.biz

Spanish Roses: Poetic Revelation of the Spanish Mystics/Ronnie Smith. —1st ed.

978-1-7356595-4-1 Hardcover
978-1-7356595-2-7 Paperback
978-1-7356595-3-4 eBook

FIRST EDITION

This book is dedicated

~ to ~

Mary, the Blessed Mother

The rose-colored light of aspiration of the soul engulfs the disciple's devotion. Mother Mary guides the "little ones" on the spiritual path to initiations administered by the Christ, represented by the vines that twine around the mystical diamond, itself an esoteric symbol of spiritual power. These spiritual initiations were witnessed by Maria of Agreda and documented in the visions of her opus, *The Mystical City of God*.

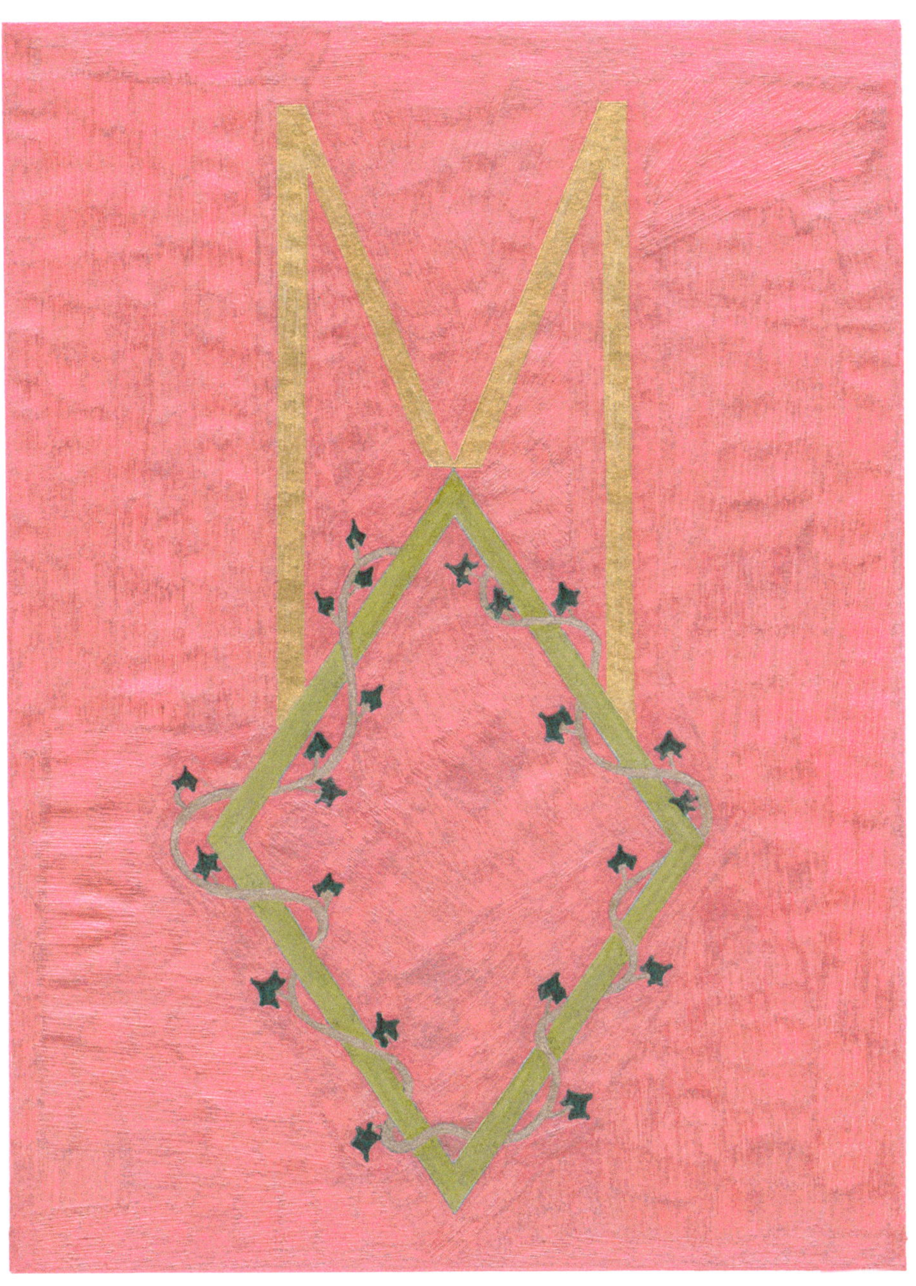

CONTENTS

Acknowledgments

I would like to express special thanks and appreciation to the people who helped make this book possible. Inspiration and the Holy Spirit are a gift, as is the help of friends. Therefore those who offered assistance, inspiration, friendship, and professionalism are dearly appreciated and remembered here: Martha Johnston, Dr. James Finley, Kathleen Sweeney, Dorothy Wilder, The Parish of Santa Ysabel Catholic Church

All interior illustrations were created by Ronnie Smith. Each one was inspired by the grace of mystical vision received in meditation.

Introduction

This is my third book of mystical poetry on the nature and lives of holy men and women who toiled in the fields of God before us. Hispanic contribution to the mystical path of Christianity is pronounced in the Spanish Golden Age of literature and the arts, the 16th and 17th centuries, where the preponderance of the saintly personages in this book lived out their lives of service. In deference to the rest of Europe, Catholic mysticism flourished throughout society during this timeframe because the Spanish held to the belief of Divine Intervention in everyday life. Therefore, mysticism impacted healing, politics, religion, literature, the arts, and social structures. One could say that the Spanish Golden Age of the arts and literature uniquely coincided with the Spanish Golden Age of Mysticism.

It has been said that throughout the ancient traditions and religions, the path to God can be summed into four interconnected paths. These are essentially the paths of Wisdom or Knowledge, Devotion, Meditation, and Service. It can be seen in the lives of these saintly Christians that their mystical paths took them into the world on one or more of these paths. The foundations of Christianity allow for all four paths. The path to God is intrinsic and a birthright for each soul, where each person is called to a holy way of life, to be "a chosen race, a royal priesthood, a holy nation" (1 Peter 2:9). Although the mystical path is a path occultly hidden in the mysteries, the Spanish mystics enunciated a way and a method.

To research the lives of these holy people, many times I 'dead ended' by the lack of translated material (Spanish into English). Other times records were poorly kept over time or destroyed during the Spanish Inquisition, which though garbed as an ecclesiastical organization, was proven in other studies outside the breadth of this book to often negotiate terms to its accused as the political extension of those in power. One will discover in certain biographical vignettes following each poem, there was overt influence and impact by the Inquisition on their work and lives. This current of influence was not exhaustively researched in the writing of this book. Suffice to say, the mere presence of the Inquisition for several hundred years in Spain and New Spain, as the Spanish American colonies were promulgated, served as a governor of religious society and in many cases as an umbrella of suppression.

Research and prayer led to an understanding of what it was like for the women to make themselves heard in the world of the Middle Ages leading into the Spanish Renaissance. Except for the more famous women such as Teresa of Avila, Ysabel of Portugal, Beatrice of Portugal, and Maria of Agreda, etc., a number of the saintly women had very little translated record of their lives. In that society of a burgeoning Renaissance, there were a couple pathways through religion for education, from which sector formal learning was available, through the clerics or monastic system. A woman of high-ranking birth could be taught to read and write by a monk. A woman with mystical gifts could, though not "a given", eventually learn to read and write via the monastery to which she was obliged through a religious order. The mystical gifts were a gateway for her to be heard. Although, abbess positions in a convent were usually held by women of high birth. Some who were not part of a formal religious order, would with like-minded women live in a house together under the rule of the nearby religious order.

These women had not taken the veil of the order as yet but chose to live in such a way. They were known as *beatas (bay-ah-tahs)*. With this way of life, these 'nuns' made sacrifices to God and to their fellow beings. This was a vocation much more preferable than the often-vulgar common life available in those times. In giving to God, they subjugated the desires of the world. This was a daily focus.

A poem dedicated to Saint James the Apostle is the entry poem. Some years ago I read *The Mystical City of God* by Abbess, Venerable Maria of Agreda. Her book of private revelation was dictated mostly to her by the Blessed Virgin Mary.

In it, she recounts the trials of St. James in his missionary journey to Spain after the crucifixion of Jesus, and before Saint James' own martyrdom back in Palestine. In Spain was built, as a result of St. James' mission, the first chapel in honor of Mother Mary at Saragossa (Zaragoza).

In this respect, the origin of Christianity in Spain was a direct result of St. James' work and Mother Mary's protection and blessing.

The design of poems in this book intends to celebrate Spanish/Hispanic spirituality given to the world. Spanish spirituality was recognized as deeply devotional and mystically gifted throughout the Spanish Golden Age. A number of my original poems are Spanish poetical forms. I chose one of these forms, the *Espinela*, to resonate throughout the book on every 8th poem.

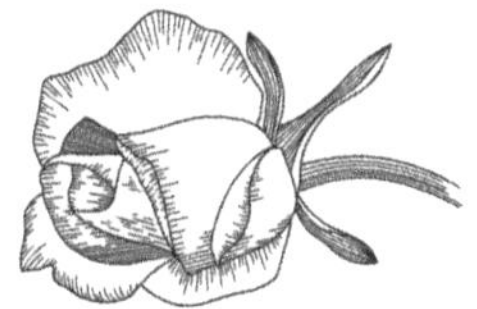

SPAIN, CIRCA 1500

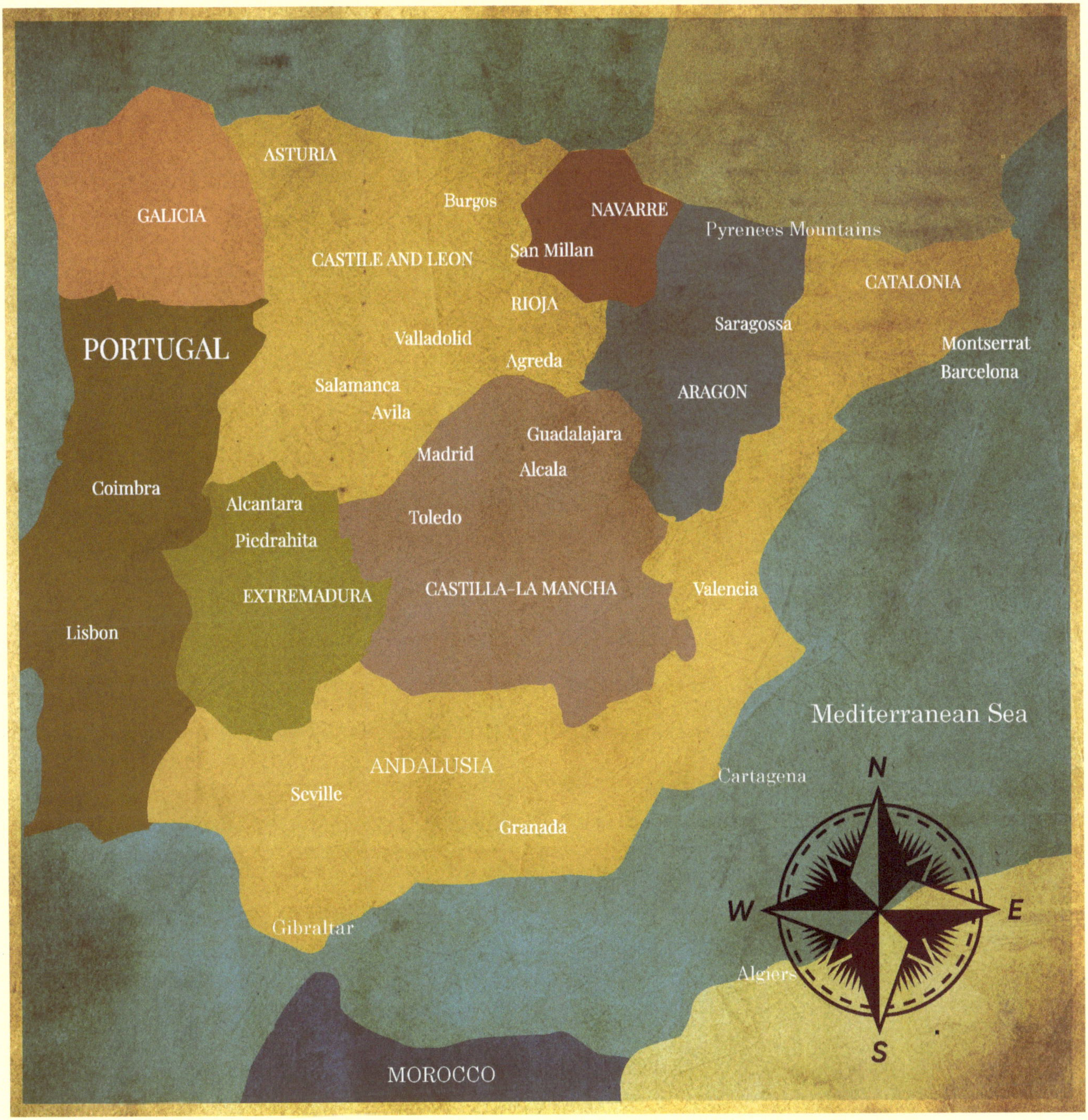

PORTUGAL
GALICIA
ASTURIA
Burgos
NAVARRE
Pyrenees Mountains
CASTILE AND LEON
San Millan
CATALONIA
RIOJA
Saragossa
Valladolid
Montserrat
Barcelona
Agreda
ARAGON
Salamanca
Avila
Guadalajara
Madrid
Alcala
Coimbra
Alcantara
Toledo
Piedrahita
EXTREMADURA
CASTILLA–LA MANCHA
Valencia
Lisbon
Mediterranean Sea
ANDALUSIA
Cartagena
Seville
Granada
Gibraltar
N
W   E
S
Algiers
MOROCCO

(AFTER MIRACLES IN GRANADA) …The heavenly Queen (Mother Mary) still more extended this favor; for She not only freed Saint James from imminent death but wished all Spain to benefit from his preaching and instruction. From Granada She ordered him to continue his journeys, commanding hundreds of her guardian angels to accompany him and show him the way from one place to another, to defend him and his disciples from all dangers, and finally, after having traversed all the provinces of Spain, to bring him to Saragossa. All this the hundred angels set about doing according to the orders of their Queen, while the rest brought Her back to Jerusalem. In such celestial company and guardianship Saint James traveled through all the Spanish realm, more securely than the Israelites through the desert. In Granada he left some of his disciples, who afterwards suffered martyrdom, and with the others and those he afterwards gathered, he continued his missionary tours in many parts of Andalusia. Then he came to Toledo, Portugal, Galicia, and Asturia. Afterwards, making digressions to different places, he arrived in Rioja, thence, passing through Lograno, he went to Toledo and Saragossa, where happened what I shall relate in the next chapter. During his peregrinations Saint James left disciples as bishops in the different cities of Spain, planting the faith and divine worship. So great and prodigious were the miracles he performed in this kingdom, that those of which we know must not appear extraordinary in comparison with those we know nothing of, since these are much more astonishing. The fruit of his preaching in Spain was immense in proportion to the shortness of his stay; and it would be a great error to say or think, that the conversions he made were few, for in all the places reached by him, he established the faith and ordained many bishops for the government of the children he engendered to Christ in this kingdom.[1]

---

1   Maria of Jesus of Agreda, *The Mystical City of God*, Marison, Fiscar (trans.), Charlotte, TAN Books, 2013.

James the Apostle (5 BC – 44 AD)

With songs of love's sacrifice, life in its toil

You sailed from Judea to farm a dry soil

Granada, you raced to replace the old air

With teachings of wisdom that counter despair

Behind the stone walls that defended the spoil

Ideals of high love were the kernels, not foil

Devotion to love has a scythe to despoil

The weeds that would choke every flower nor spare

The songs of love's sacrifice

Apostles of love bring the holiest oil

The dauntless stand up to the greed in the roil

And mystics hold fast to a dream alto-rare

As Mary urged James with the angels to care

For souls of the saints who will never recoil

From songs of love's sacrifice

Solar Angel

Painted in memory of Mrs. Angeline Bork, the *Solar Angel* is the expression of the soul's journey through life on earth. The ego of the personality is purified by God through selfless deeds (the white figure at the bottom), freely offering one's spiritual gifts to the world. In turn, spiritual growth matures as the soul builds its contributions to the Tree of Life. Final liberation through physical death and eventual ascension is via the solar angel (as a purified soul), depicted here as the golden angel at the top of the tree. Encasing this process through life is the divine love of God (the large heart-shape) radiating to all. In this case, the domain of the Blessed Virgin Mary whose rose-colored light represents her aura of power of divine love, guides those who belong to Her.

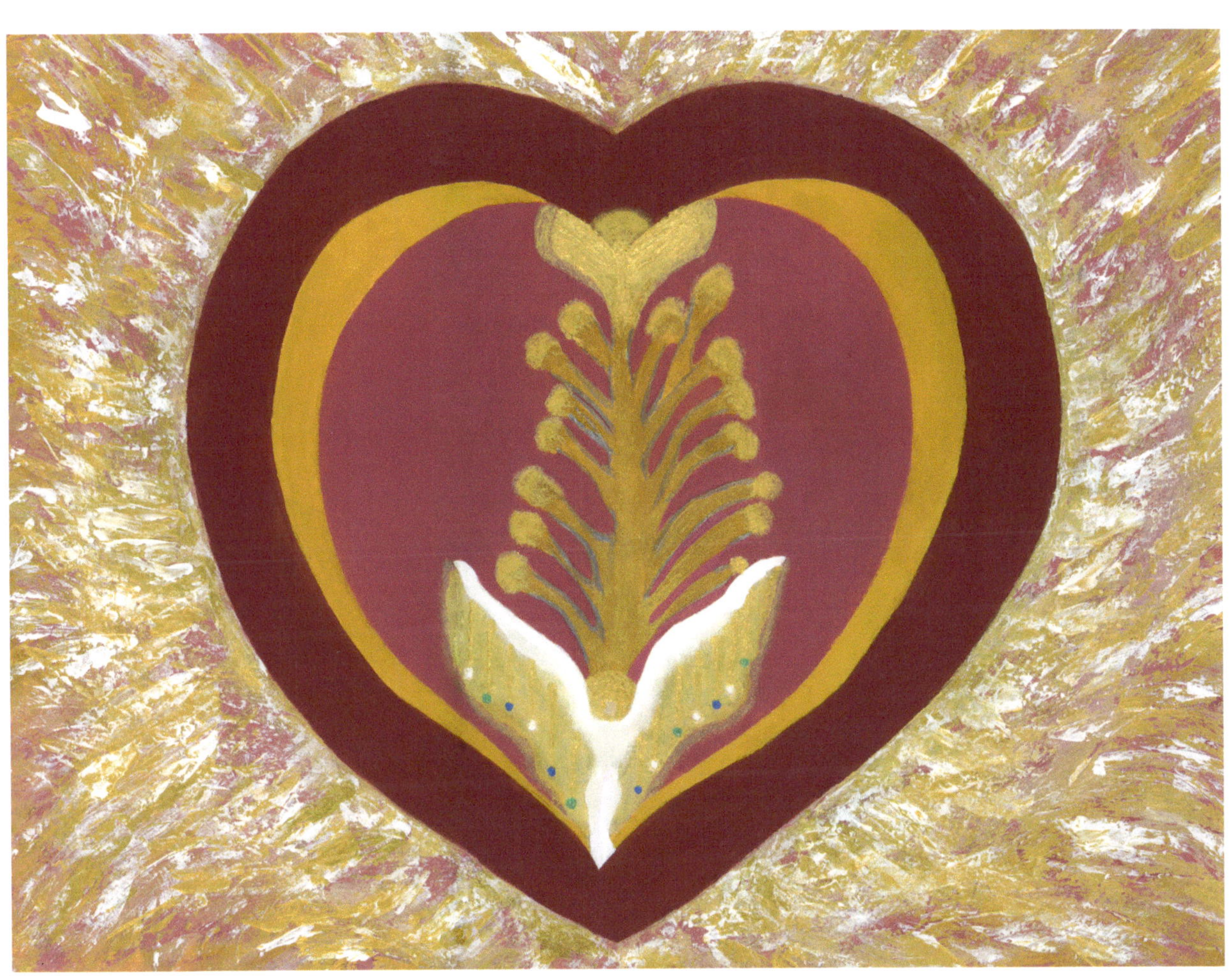

SAINT TERESA WAS OF merchant class parentage and had a good early life. She lost her mother at eleven years of age, and in her grief decided to assume the Blessed Virgin Mary as her spiritual mother. This profoundly affected her life, as she chose to become a nun and later reform the Carmelite Order after a very popular social life in her youth. Despite the constant monitor of the Spanish Inquisition, she went on to become a most celebrated Renaissance writer on mysticism in Spain, and either founded or influenced the founding of some 40 convents and monasteries. She was later canonized and declared a Doctor of the Church.[2]

---

2   Teresa of Avila, *The Life of Teresa of Jesus*, Peers, E. Allison, New York, Doubleday, 2004.

Teresa of Avila (1515-1582)

When I could sense the love that lights the day
I saw there was a glow in every thing
Where angels come to life and lions lay

My childhood died when mother couldn't stay
The song of Holy Mary I would sing
For children sense the love that lights the day

The visions of my ecstasies allay
The struggles that my order was to bring
Where angels come to life and lions lay

And with the Carmelites I strode The Way
Reform, Reform, was not just any fling
For I could sense the love that lights the day

In mansions of the heart I sought to pray
Celestial wisdom, my engagement ring
As angels come to life where lions lay

As nuptial mystics step through walls of clay
To edify a church despite its sting
These children sense the love that lights the day
Where angels come to life and lions lay

JOHN OF THE CROSS was born into poverty. He later became a Carmelite monk after completing his education. He was "recruited" into the reformed order of the Discalced Carmelites by Teresa of Avila. He helped establish that male order under great persecution in which he was imprisoned, by his own order, and beaten daily for over a year. He eventually escaped and brought to life his revelations and writings.

After his death he was recognized perhaps as the leading mystical and theological writer and poet of the Spanish Renaissance at its peak. The Catholic Church canonized him and declared him a Doctor of the Church. Upon his death bed, he asked his nurse/nun to read from (the Christian Bible) the Song of Songs. He is recorded to have whispered with his dying breath, "What beautiful daisies…".[3]

---

3   Herrara, R. A., *Silent Music*, William B. Eerdmans Publishing Company, Grand Rapids, 2004.

John of the Cross (1542-1591)

Las Margaritas (The Daisies)

I watch the stars that torch the gulf of night
Reflections of the Logos' wondrous might
And I, inside this jail to ride a whale
With tailfin that will fan the distant glows
Of thousand-million-sun celestial floes

In youth I saw with eyes both new and raw
I loved the leaves and wind and leapt the law
My tiny frame, like willows not so frail
Had spirit blowing through the graceful strings
Devotion's hanging harp until it sings

When daisies spring from meadows, not a hoe
The ones we do not trample, they will grow
And if we take up silence on the trail
Discarding weeds becomes our daily plight
And nothingness transforms the inward blight

When heaven calls there's nothing I can bring
The road of nothing opens for one thing
The Knower knows a grace that will not fail
That barricades the world with hallowed awe
For every sacred daisy that I saw

Luis de Leon was a Spanish lyric poet, Augustinian friar, theologian and academic, active during the Spanish Golden age. He had an illustrious academic career which included many notable writings. His career was marked midway through by false accusations of heretical writing, proposed by other Dominican professors before the Inquisition. After spending four years in prison at Valladolid, Spain, in which under poor conditions he continued writing, he returned to Salamanca in triumph and rose to the top of his field.[4]

Here is a writer of the first rank—perhaps the greatest of Spain's poets and certainly one of her leading prose writers, who devotes powers which would have given his treatment of any theme distinction to the supreme theme of the soul's quest for God. Not that that quest was by any means his only preoccupation. In his poems … (he) extolls moderation and comfort, or a lover of Nature or of music. The mystical ideas of Luis de Leon are latent in a few of his poems… and are expanded more fully and clearly in *The Names of Christ*… *The Names of Christ* has much to say of the mystical life, contains some eloquent descriptions of characteristic mystical states and occasionally looks forward to the mystic's ultimate goal.[5]

Posterity has pronounced the final word. His prose works are immortal. His poems have placed him at the highest pinnacle of literary fame. We honor him for his integrity, the generosity and nobility of his character, his fair-mindedness, his self-forgetful championship of the defenseless and weak, his loyalty, his devotion to his friends, the grandeur of his personality. We place him among the greatest of men.[6]

---

4 Luis de Leon, *Wikipedia*, 20 April 2022, Web accessed 3 July 2022. https://en.wikipedia.org/wiki/Luis_de_León

5 Peers, E. Allison, *The Mystics of Spain*, London, George Allen & Unwin Ltd., 1951.

6 Sister Felicia, O.S.A., *Seven Spanish Mystics*, Cambridge, Massachusetts, Shea Brothers Press, 1947.

LUIS DE LEON (1528-1591)

You're a poet of dreams, my son
Who must vanish with Venus to dry desert air
To add ink of pink light to decorate dusk
And your pen with the henna of Mother Earth
Will reflect Sublimity's subtle union
And tap its silo to seed the world
With kinetic words that burst with lightning
To blind an intellect stirring to Wonder

You're the sower of stars, little one
Exude your tales from spores of nova
That tiny lives may know celestial splay
Of Those who chandelier great lights
From cosmic planes of Divinity
Splashing hues the breadth of vast silences
To reach and wash, to adorn the way
From the heart of a Logos in perpetual glory

You're the pathfinder of sacred waters
For a cleft in the rock opens inward
To the womb of its spring in the deepest mount
Where you drink and get drunk on pure truth
Which seasons lead jars of reason, belief
Religion, tradition, and dungeon
Your tongue may lap at the pool of nothingness
The mirror of a sun aflame forever

Mystical Marriage

Mystical marriage, nuptial mystics, spiritual marriage, and espousal to Christ is a relationship in Christian spirituality where the disciple/devotee lives intimately united to God through grace and love (2 Cor 11:2). This painting was inspired by a vision received in meditation of Maria of Agreda.

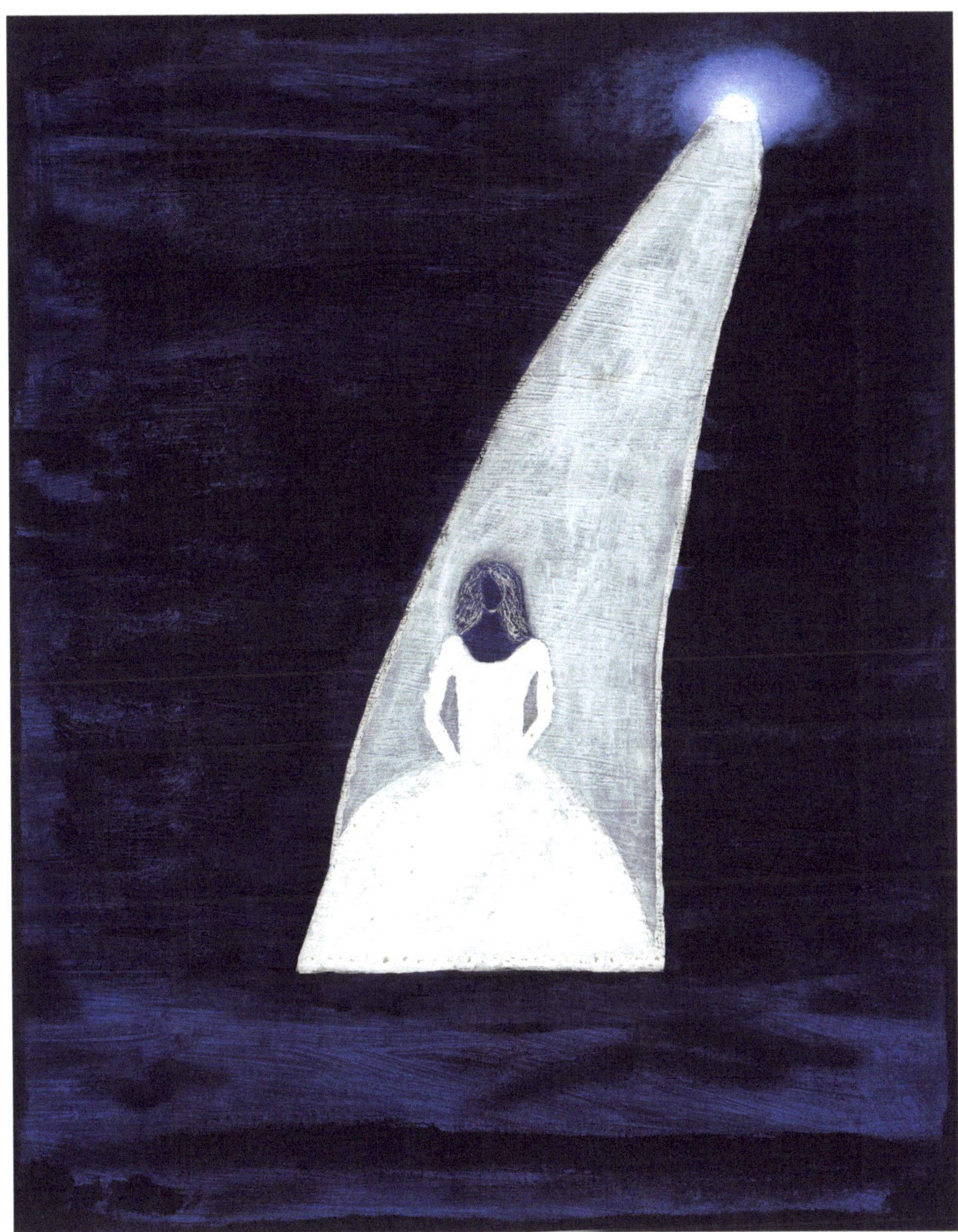

MARIA OF AGREDA, KNOWN as the Lady in Blue for the color of her nun's garment, was an abbess and author of 12 books. Her most notable to date is the *Mystical City of God,* which was dictated to her by the Blessed Mother Mary. She was instrumental in influencing church dogma of the Immaculate Conception. She counseled and mentored King Philip IV of Spain, exchanging over 600 letters with him, thus influencing states and nations. At 19 she began over 500 out-of-body journeys to the New World to teach and help the American Indian tribes of the American Southwest. These bilocations have been documented on both sides of the Atlantic. She never physically left her convent in Agreda, Spain and is celebrated in New Mexico, Oklahoma, and Texas. Miracles are attributed to her.[7]

Pools and holy wells have long been a medium of God's healing throughout arcane and modern sacred history. For centuries the pool of Bethesda (in Hebrew, lit. "house of mercy") was a spring-fed pool inside the Sheep Gate of Jerusalem. It was believed to have supernatural powers of healing. It was also believed that if a sick person entered the pool the moment after an angel of the pool stirred it, the person would be healed. See also John 5: 2-9.[8]

---

7   Fedewa, Marilyn H., *Maria of Agreda: Mystical Lady in Blue,* Albuquerque, University of New Mexico Press, 2009.

8   John the Apostle, *New American Bible, revised edition,* Washington, DC, Confraternity of Christian Doctrine, Inc., 2010.

Maria of Agreda (1602-1665)

The Woman at the Well

Once I crawled through the crowd to her holy pool

With the hope that my body would galvanize

Or a wing-beating angel might soothe and cool

In the darkening evening my burning thighs

Like a tern on a beach, whom the winds unbind

To American wilds she was freed in youth

For the tribes she would teach with a fearless mind

Wove the reeds of nobility's endless truth

Then I begged at her abbey for broth and food

As her sweetness gave hope to a throng so ill

In her bastion of love lives a homeless brood

In that stronghold compassion is living still

Her elixir of life I shall drink like this

From the cup of her hands at the well of bliss

DIEGO DE ESTELLA WAS a Franciscan mystic and theologian. Born in Estella, Navarre and died in Salamanca, in the present-day autonomous community of Castile and Leon.

(He was) a pure ascetic…in his *Book of the Vanity of the World*, which belongs to the history of mysticism by virtue of his *Devout Meditations on the Love of God*, which immediately after publication went into three more editions and is still being re-published today. The *Meditations* are essentially a 'Book of the Lover and the Beloved'… and it is by the lover that it will be most read.[9]

---

9   Peers, E. Allison, *The Mystics of Spain*, London, George Allen & Unwin Ltd., 1951.

DIEGO DE ESTELLA (1524-1578)
LOVER AND BELOVED

I sought her, heedless of the heights beyond Everest

From the lowlands I have glimpsed her beauty

And now leave my dull lives that groped in wasteland

To chant solstice-long songs of our highest love

Through her flowering tree blows silent wind

Where I gather blush petals with the scent of God

For her love is a round-eyed girl who would hide

When I was so young and raged through the mountains

She returned with a locket of dew from afar

That would drench my eyes with her opulent innocence

Her lily, my heart, is veiled in the mist

But will glisten when morning sings with light

As the peaks of great massifs slide to the deep

Into waves that scroll in the fizz of foam

I shall swim the dark sea over curves of the Earth

To elope with one hope to our verdant isle

I shall plant our white love in an orchard of holiness

Whose blooms turn to swans that will fly in rapture

Maria of Ajofrin became an Hieronymite nun after first living as a *beata* (bay ah' tah); a lay woman who made a private vow of chastity and followed a religious rule, living under the same roof with other like women. She had several mystical, well-known experiences, including a wound that appeared on her forehead and chest and bled during Holy Mass. Via visions of the blessed Virgin Mary and Jesus, this led to stern reform in the clergy in Toledo, Spain, and extirpation of heresy.[10]

The nuptial mystics, so named, envisioned betrothal to God as the high state of divine union. Other famous Spanish nuptial mystics include John of the Cross and Teresa of Avila.

The Hieronymite nuns, founded in 1375 by Maria Garcias, also became numerous throughout the Iberian peninsula.[11]

10 Surtz, Ronald, *Writing Women in Late Medieval and Early Modern Spain: The Mothers of Saint Teresa of Avila*, Philadelphia, University of Pennsylvania Press, 1995.

11 Butler, Edward Cuthbert, *Hieronymites*, Wikipedia, 27 March 2022. Web accessed September 2, 2022. https://en.wikipedia.org/wiki/Hieronymites

Maria of Ajofrin (c.1455-1489)

The Beata

Her wounds became a nuptial cake for life
For love must give its portion to the poor
A girl became beata then a wife

The clay of souls is framed by potter's knife
And winds will lift the waves to rake the shore
Her wounds became a nuptial cake for life

Within the church the rotten fruit was rife
A sign of blood reforms, if to restore
A girl became beata then a wife

For decades I had labored under strife
Incessantly my banner flew for war
My wounds became a nuptial cake for life

Her battles dabbed her like a palette knife
Then she became the art instead of gore
A girl became beata then a wife

The scars that mark the cross to afterlife
Will stand like runes that love will underscore
Her wounds became a nuptial cake for life
A girl became beata then a wife

JUAN DIEGO WAS A Chichimec peasant who was exceptionally devout to God through the Church. He and his wife, María Lucía, were initially baptized by the Franciscan missionaries who arrived in Mexico from Spain in 1524. Thus, his religious sanctity was already strong before having four (4) apparitions of the Blessed Virgin Mary. During the course of the apparitions over several days, Juan Diego attempted to convince the local bishop that the Virgin Mary wanted him to erect a chapel at Tepeyac Hill in her honor to heal and help the local devout. In returning to the bishop with flowers from the hill at Mother Mary's request, Bishop Juan Bernardino saw that the Holy Virgin produced a magnificently colored image of herself on Juan Diego's mantle (*tilma*), without Juan Diego realizing it had been done. After the apparitions, Juan Diego lived next to the hermitage at Tepeyac. He devoutly served the Virgin Mary the rest of his life at the erected shrine. The mantle is venerated today with many associated miracles. Eventually the Basilica of Our Lady of Guadeloupe was built at that site, where it is now a major world pilgrimage for tens of millions each year.[12]

[*Cuauhtlatoatzin (Chichimec)*: he is who speaks like an eagle.]

---

12 Badde, Paul, *Maria of Guadalupe: Shaper of History, Shaper of Hearts*, Ignatius Press, San Francisco, 2009.

Juan Diego Cuauhtlatoatzin (1474–1548), an Espinela

When eagles speak, Creation heeds

For when I hear the One I seek

A raptor, I, can feed the weak

Whose cities burn from wanton deeds

The flight of love is flight that leads

To higher love, to underlay

That love of Mary is my way

Which lifts me over mountain vale

To mount the winds and glide a gale

To rodeo this life today

(Pedro Malon) went to Salamanca to study letters but entered the convent of Augustinians of Cascante and afterwards professed solemn vows on October 27, 1557. In university he was a disciple of Fray Luis de Leon and Fr. Juan de Guevara, which influenced him deeply. Pedro Malon was reluctant to publish his works under the suppressive atmosphere of the Inquisition in view of the difficulties that had also suffered his master Fray Luis de Leon. He was, therefore, in the convent of Saragossa, where he was prior (1575-1577), and in Huesca (1578-1583), also as prior. In this stay, he began to compose his works. At the University of Huesca he got his doctorate in Theology in 1581. In 1582 he was appointed teacher of the Augustinian Order and in 1583, being the definitor of the province, he was appointed professor in Zaragoza. He took part in the foundation of the monastery of Our Lady of Loreto, in Huesca, Aragon, in 1585. He became prior of the convent of Barcelona. In 1588 he published his only printed book, *The Conversion of the Magdalene.*[13]

---

13 Pedro Malon de Chaide, *Wikipedia*, 31 January 2022, Web accessed 13 July 2022. https://en.wikipedia.org/wiki/Pedro_Mal%C3%B3n_de_Chaide (modified)

Pedro Malon de Chaide (1530-1589)

Ode to Love-Wisdom

I sift for blue worlds in a sandglass of spheres

I've saddled this planet, my bronco through time

To chronicle Beauty that rules with one rhyme

I'm lassoing suns with the rope of light-years

As love fills the wisdom on down to genome

And rises to clouds that will everywhere roam

Your grandfather oaks cradle wisdom that flows

Through veins of the earth, to a forest that knows

I know neither God, nor of what God's about

I'm dumb to the Cosmos that love has carved out

Unspeakable love I can only reflect

With whom shall I wade into Arctic-white snows?

With Whom the great stars are but waterfall floes

In caverns of indigo mists will perfect

In mystery love blows invisible breeze

Caressing the miniscule creatures and seas

The touch of an angel attends an elm

My breastplate of sunrise illumines their realm

An aegis of love from the Mother of Lights

And mark of the angels a lover unites

(MARIA JUSTA) WAS BORN in La Victoria de Acentejo on the north of the island of Tenerife in the Spanish Canary Islands. She trained as a Franciscan in the Saint Joseph Convent in La Orotava. Her life was involved in mysticism and controversy. The Holy Inquisition tried her as a witch. She was accused of practicing Molinist doctrines. It was hinted that the relationship with her confessor was not appropriate for a religious person. Her biographer and confessor, Andrés de Abreu, burned the biography he had written about her.

However, Dominican friar Jose Herrera said that among her virtues was to give sight to the blind, to make the deaf hear, the mute to speak, heal the lame, heal diseases, and expel demons.

Sr. Maria Justa healed the sick by transferring to her person the evils and diseases that afflicted them. Shamanic priests in other cultures used analogous techniques to cure convalescents. That similarity fed the suspicions of those who called her an *alumbrada*. During these healings, the nun suffered multiple ailments, covering her body in sores, and elevating her body temperature, which brought her to the brink of death. According to the chronicles of the time, her body showed signs of sanctity, such as flexibility, pleasant fragrances and fluidity of her blood. After her death, the Franciscan Order in the Canary Islands conducted a process of canonization that was later halted. Her case was ascribed to the phenomenon of the *Alumbrados* that arose in small Castilian towns two centuries earlier. These … doctrines considered heretical by the Catholic Church, believing that union with God came only through mystical experiences and private prayer, without the need for Church sacraments.[14]

---

14 María Justa de Jesús, *Wikipedia*, 19 June 2022, Web accessed 21 July 2022.

https://en.wikipedia.org/wiki/Sister_Mar%C3%ADa_Justa_de_Jesús

Maria Justa de Jesus (1667-1723)

There's an island where waves will embark from the shore

They will carry one love from the heart of The All

As it dilates the world with a balm that is pure

As a girl she was drawn by a convent's allure

For the way of a healer begins with a crawl

There's an island where waves will embark from the shore

And the winds of the ocean may sting and endure

For my wineskins are filled with both fruit and the gall

As I dilate the world with a balm that is pure!

To adventure the seas is a life that wants more

The long journey with God can reap more than a trawl

There's an island where waves will embark from the shore

Let the works of true love reach the rich and the poor

For a mystical love is not blocked by a wall

As it dilates the world with a balm that is pure

There's a light that an evil will try to obscure

But to shine is a choice of the soul and its call

There's an island where waves will embark from the shore

As they dilate the world with a balm that is pure

ESSENTIALLY, SAINT AMUNIA (ALSO Amunna) of San Millán was a Benedictine hermit, from what is currently La Rioja province in Northern Spain. She became a hermit after the death of her husband, following her daughter, Saint Aurea, who was also a hermit. Both saints spent their contemplative lives at the Monastery of San Millan de la Cogolla. Gonzalo de Berceo, considered the first poet of the Spanish language, wrote an account of her (Aurea) life called the *Vida de Santa Oria*.[15]

Aurea (also Auria; Oria) was born near Mansilla, six leagues (18 miles) from St. Emiliano (San Millan). Auria was given to piety, charity, and asceticism from her earliest years. She took the veil when young and went to live with some women of kindred tastes, in a retreat adjoining the Benedictine monastery of St. Emiliano de Suso, according to the custom of the time, which permitted a community of consecrated virgins to live near a house for monks. She was favored with celestial visions, and the fame of her sanctity spread over all the country. The abbot and two monks attended her death bed. Her mother was also present and died a few days after her. A sepulcher was hewn for her in the rock, and there she and her mother were buried. Their tomb… was to be seen some hundreds of years afterwards, in the Church of St. Emiliano de Suso. Sandovellius adds that the town of Soria on the Douro (Durium) near the ruins of Numantia is a contraction of Saint Oria and is so called from this saint.[16]

---

15 Saint Amunia de Millan, *Wikipedia*, 28 March 2022, Web accessed 25 June 2022.

   https://en.wikipedia.org/wiki/Amunia_of_San_Millán

16 Dunbar, Agnes B.C., *A Dictionary of Saintly Women, Vol. I*, London, George Bell & Sons, 1904.

Amunia (c. 1020-1070) and Aurea (1043-1070) of San Millan

A mother and a daughter found a home
The victor, death, scrapes victims from the poor
The mount that hermits clamber, angels comb

When refugees for love are forced to roam
The willow tree that bends speaks something more
A mother and a daughter found a home

A suddenness of light can follow gloam
The visions in the night begin to soar
The mount that hermits clamber, angels comb

The fields will sprinkle flowers mixed with brome
A meadow we might find behind a door
A mother and a daughter found a home

A mystic teacher lights the temple's dome
The Trinity is mystically the lure
The mount that hermits clamber, angels comb

The light that leads to love will polychrome
The tree that greets the sun and seeds the shore
A mother and a daughter found a home
The mount that hermits clamber, angels comb

ELIZABETH (ISABEL, YSABEL) OF Portugal, also known as Elizabeth (Isabella) of Aragon, Spain was also called by the people, *Rainha Santa* (Portuguese; lit. Queen Saint, i.e. holy queen). She was named after her aunt, Queen (Saint) Elizabeth of Hungary. She was betrothed to King Denis of Portugal at age 12 and formally became queen at 17. She spent her life caring for the poor, even at a young age when she displayed the miracle of the roses. That miracle informed a much older king, who had suspected her of taking food or money to give to the poor, hidden in the folds of her dress. When he questioned her about the hidden contents, she opened her dress to reveal a flourish of roses. She made peace between kings and royal family on several occasions, avoiding bloodshed and derision in the kingdoms. She was a mystic and was accompanied by miracles of healing when she spent her last years at the convent in Coimbra, Portugal.[17]

---

17 McNabb, Vincent, *St. Elizabeth of Portugal*, Las Vegas, Mediatrix Press, 2015.

Ysabel of Portugal (1271-1336)

Holy Queen

Your royal mantle shielded us from fear
A younger you would shine through windows bare
And later your unswerving sun arose
No king could keep you towered far away

We welcomed you, who brought such solace here
Who thwarted spilling blood that would not spare
Our lives that ransomed battlefields in rows
Of armies you left staring down the day

We grappled drought and famine with your cheer
We stole your smile that lifted our despair
When spirit's river flowed through you and rose
Our hearts would buoy hoping you would stay

Your convent's calm was healing when we'd hear
Your heart that sang for souls with mother's care
For from your gown fell every scented rose
Whose oil for hearts would mend and aches allay

For you, my throat, athirst like panting deer
Who leap and lunge ravines for mountain air
I'll sprint the winds that ripple with the roes
Through highland vales that meadow golden hay

MEDITATION ON THE MYSTICAL ROSE

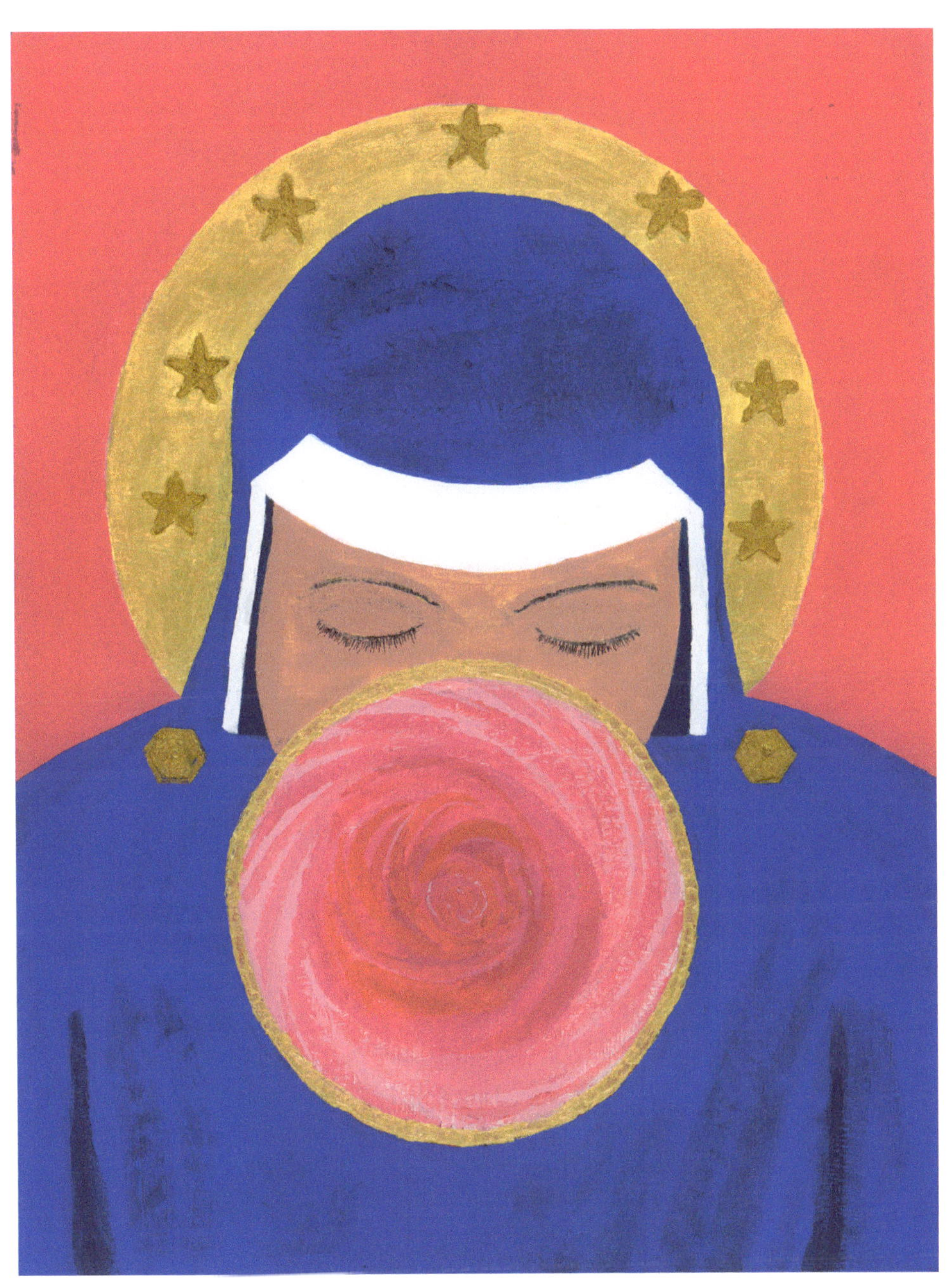

The Mystical Rose

While meditating, a vision of a single rose (mystical rose) appeared with an image of the Blessed Virgin Mary resting behind it. The next day in prayer, while praying the Litany to the Blessed Virgin Mary, at the phrase, "Mystical Rose, pray for us", the vision from the previous day returned and I began to receive the teaching of the vision

The Mystical Rose is a sign of union with the Blessed Mother. Oneness is what Mother Mary desires for the disciple of Hers. Mother Mary said, "You should always desire union with Me. Focusing on the Mystical Rose brings one into union with God. If you are in union with God, you are in union with Me. There is only One love. An all-pervasive radiance of God that you now are capable of consciously connecting to. You have been given such experiences like the drive into southern Missouri that day, or on the beach at Baile Shear, Outer Hebrides. Don't let the mind take you into subterranean paths of separateness. Don't let the emotions and its desire component take you away from the state of consciousness of the One love."

"The Mystical Rose is the pattern of divine life, and therefore of your life as a soul seeking to express your God-given divinity as you are created in the image of God."

"The rose is the perfection of beauty in the plant kingdom. At this peak (of evolution) its beauty exudes attraction; its scent is the highly developed quality which is in the nature of the divine energy of love. This ray of love, as an energy, magnetically holds matter and therefore the Cosmos together. This is part of the One love of which I previously spoke. … identifying with it behooves your growth. Memorize its qualities. They are to be manifested."

ACCORDING TO THE MOST ancient biographical news …, provided by Sister Juana San Miguel, who formed part of the first community of the Order of the Immaculate Conception. Beatrice was the founder of the Order of the Immaculate Conception. She was of royal lineage in Portugal and found her way to be a Lady in waiting for Isabel the Queen of Castile. Because of her great beauty she was imprisoned by the queen's irrational jealousy. After three days spent in a small cell, she was released after fully entrusting her safety to the Blessed Virgin Mary, who appeared to her in prison. She was told she would start a new order dedicated to the Immaculate Conception. Later, after she returned to court life, she abandoned it for the monastery of Santo Domingo El Real in Toledo. Here, she did not join an order. She lived a penitent, holy life as a *beata* in the monastery. After 30-plus years, she and her group of like-minded nuns were given a new place called the Palace of Galiana by the Catholic Queen Isabel to establish an order dedicated to the Virgin Mary of the Immaculate Conception. (Beatrice is said to have had mystical experiences throughout her life).[18]

---

18 Sister Juana San Miguel, "Saint Beatriz de Silva", *Maria de Jesus de Agreda, Mariadeagreda.org*, accessed 10 July 2022, https://mariadeagreda.org/en/franciscan-conceptionist/saint-beatriz-de-silva/#

Beatrice da Silva (1424-1492)

Sonnet for a Spanish Rose

The rose holds designs of what beauty can be

As streams that gloss stones through a forest and field

I seek the cold springs that the mountains have sealed

In lakes full of sky that let God alone see

I plant a pink rose that is pruned by a queen

Her mystical love is the rain and the snow

The patience of seasons are lessons that grow

Eternity's petals in spirals pristine

The Cosmos created the rose with its scent

Its essence awakens the heart of the strong

Its nature of love is magnetic and meant

To pull to its whirlpool the many who throng

For waters of love, as true love won't relent

To swirl into life as it lifts us along

SON OF THE GOVERNOR of a castle, Alonso studied music and served as choir boy in the cathedral at Toledo, Spain for three years. He attended the University of Salamanca, Spain at age 14 and was a spiritual student of Saint Thomas of Villanova. He became a priest and served as Augustinian Prior in Seville. His missionary work in Mexico ended shortly when he could not overcome severe arthritis. Returning to Spain, Alonso became preacher to the court of King Charles V, sometime after 1549. He refused to accept the standard royal stipends and lived as a humble monk. His door was always open to anyone seeking spiritual guidance. His free time was spent visiting the sick in hospital, prisoners in jail, and the poor living on the street. He had a great devotion to the Virgin Mary. He helped found Augustinian monasteries and convents, and to advance reforms within the order.[19]

He wrote numerous treatises, and his *Mount of Contemplation* described the mystic's path and way of life. At his funeral, the people of Madrid, as testified by Quevedo, filed past the chapel of rest and rushed the doors of the church of the college, knocking down the doors seeking some relic, a splinter of the bed, or a fragment of his clothes, his shoes or of his hair shirt.[20]

---

19 Saint Alonso de Orozco Mena, *CatholicSaints.Info.*, 18 May 2022. Web Accessed 14 June 2022. http://catholicsaints.info/saint-alonso-de-orozco-mena/

20 Alonso de Orozco, Vatican News Services, 19 May 2002. Web accessed 17 June 2022. https://www.vatican.va/news_services/liturgy/2002/documents/ns_lit_doc_20020519_orozco_en.html#top

Alonso de Orozco (1500-1591)

Religious, simple life you led, our friend
A candle used to light your room left stark
Your pen amended minds and made its mark
Determined son of Mary to the end

A life of love we'll one day comprehend
It launches us from lands we must embark
The Spanish Golden Age was just an ark
To voyage what a mystic must transcend

Fresh waters cooled the fevers of the lost
The thunderclap of love brings healing rain
What gift you gave to inmates won't exhaust
As rivers give their wealth to feed the plain
From castle to the street your life embossed
The love of God that God cannot constrain

CASILDA WAS A DAUGHTER of a Moorish king of Toledo, who held Christians captive in his prison. Casilda could see them from her windows in the palace. She had a brother named Alimaymon who was converted to Christianity and to whom the Blessed Virgin Mary appeared in a place called Nuestra Senora de Sepetran. His conversion led to that of his sister, who joined him in his charitable work alleviating the sufferings of the Christian prisoners and slaves. Her official conversion came when she requested to travel north into Christian territory to the Lake of San Vicente, near Burgos, to try to get healed from the dysentery she suffered. At Burgos she recovered and was baptized in the church of St. Vincent. She would not return to Toledo but remained among the Christians and lived as a religious recluse in a hut on the banks of the lake. Miracles took place in her life in Toledo and Burgos.[21]

---

21 Dunbar, Agnes B.C., *A Dictionary of Saintly Women, Vol. I*, London, George Bell & Sons, 1904.

Casilda of Toledo (950-1050)

My robes and my maidens would brighten the court

I fed the bound Christians, the slaves of the fort

These goods of the king could be sold to Algiers

Their youth would be lost as mortality nears

In hearts there are rooms for the love we forgot

For God is the love and the mansion, the lot

Divinity spares an unending pure stream

Connecting the worlds of both near and extreme

I lived on a lake where the sun and moon dream

I blessed the white mountains and sloughs of rich bream

My refuge in God saved my life, left to rot

My gift to the children of Mary was not

My eyes see the magic my spirit reveres

Invisible prayer is the faith of the seers

A bay full of dolphins can easily sport

How love and elation around us cavort

OF NOBLE BIRTH, *FRAY* (Brother) Bernardino grew up in Seville and became a page to an exiled Portuguese nobleman (Duke Álvaro of Portugal) in that city. He studied medicine, possibly graduating from the University of Seville, and began to practice as a physician around 1507. In 1510, though, a close friend entered the Order of Saint Francis as a lay brother, and he did the same. He remained a lay brother in the Franciscan order for the next thirty years, for most of that time living in the friary of San Francisco del Monte, near Villaverde del Río, a town about eighteen miles north-east of Seville.

De Laredo is most remembered for his spiritual treatise entitled, *Ascent of Mount Sion (Subida del Monte Sión)*. By introducing Teresa of Avila to the prayer of quiet, she credits her reading of *Ascent of Mount Sion* for helping her deal with her perplexity caused by, on the one hand, her inability to meditate, and on the other hand, by supernatural experiences she was undergoing.[22]

---

22 Bernardino de Laredo, *The Ascent of Mount Sion*, E. Allison Peers, London, Faber & Faber, 1952.

Bernardino de Laredo (1482-1540), an Espinela

In the sickbay you healed and prayed

Over lambs you would soon relax

Though disease in the limbs would tax

The young faith that a monk displayed

Your instruction, true son, obeyed

The one law, the clear way to light

Through a suffering servant's night

And allowed, in the silence, loss

Of an ego who lugs a cross

Across desert, the soul's great plight

FAR FROM BEING IGNORANT or uncultivated, he (Juan) had been trained, like his great compatriot Luis de Leon, in Salamanca and in Alcala, and was solidly grounded in the classical and theological studies of the day. He so distinguished himself in his student days as to earn the title of "the Master." He became a great preacher and could hold listeners intent and receptive however lengthy his discourse. The Bishop of Seville set him…to spiritual ministration throughout… Andalusia. "Apostle to Andalusia" has become, therefore, his usual title. But he also earned the title of "Father of the Spanish Saints." One of those holy and humble men of old, he was himself so saintly that he could assist Saint Ignatius in the foundation of the Society (of Jesus) and become the spiritual guide of saints so exalted as Saint Teresa, Saint Francis Borgia, Fray Luis de Granada, and Saint Peter of Alcantara. It was he to whom Saint Teresa submitted her autobiography. He left us numerous works from his pen.[23]

---

23 Sister Felicia, O.S.A., *Seven Spanish Mystics*, Cambridge, Massachusetts, Shea Brothers Press, 1947.

Juan de Avila (1500-1569)

A hermit can offer you desert and sea

Or story the seasons of figs on a tree

At times I have sweltered in sun with no flight

An owl on a fir in the dusk is just right

Apostle and Father, both gave me a name

I wore a priest's cloth, but a cloth just the same

Beneath my drab cowl was a body quite slight

My owl was in hiding of sunrise too bright

If knowledge was wisdom, how wise we would be

Mistakes are a tutor, no wisdom is free

The truth has a cliff with a rope to hold tight

The owl hoots the truth from an oak out of sight

On treks I could sup from the vines of that day

The earthly and lowly were strewn on the way

The brilliance of love and of God, is one light

An owl shines through eyes from the lattice of night

THE CHAPEL OF THE BLESSED MOTHER

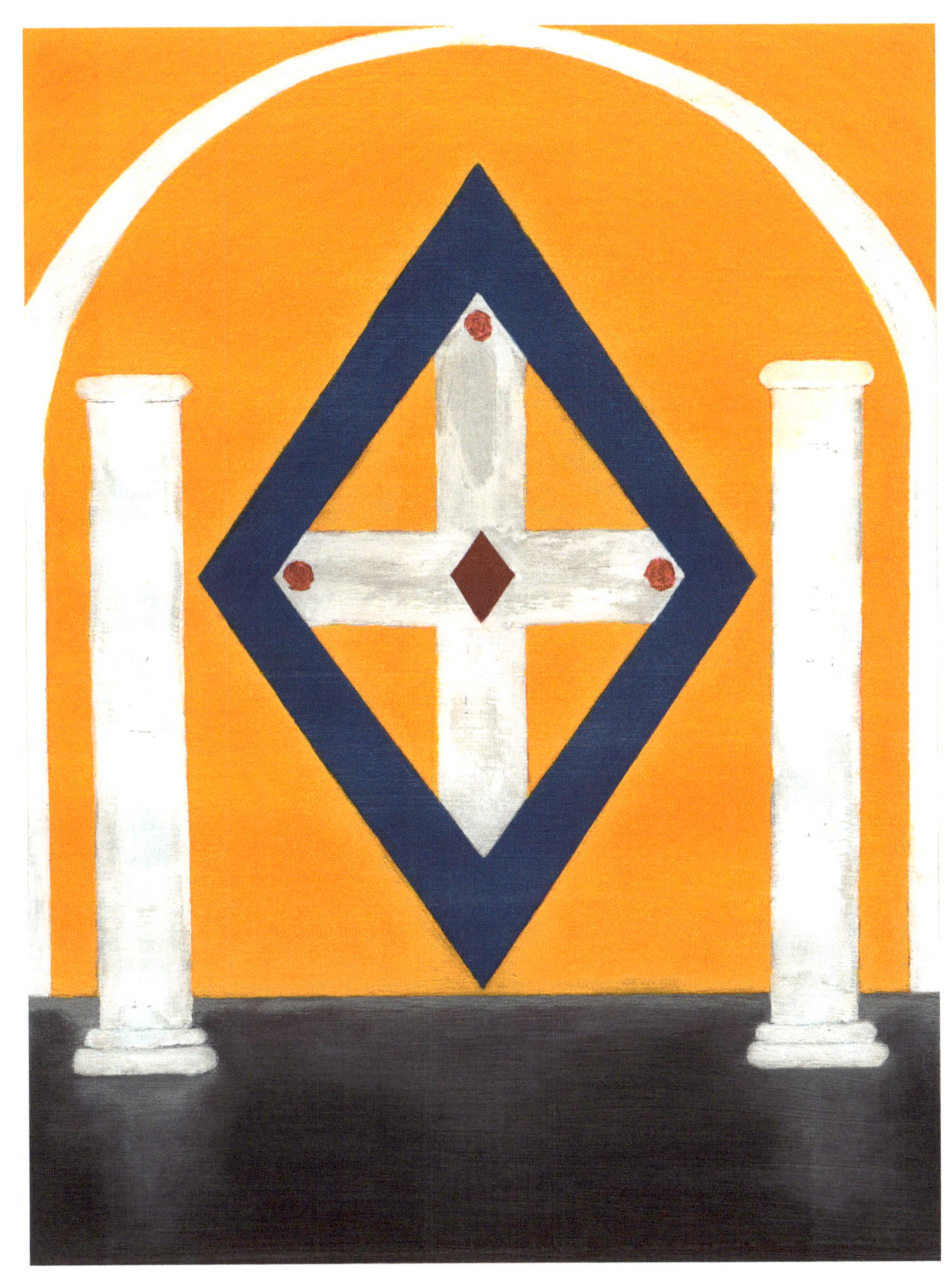

GROWING UP IN THE town of Granada, Spain, Luis became well known for his sanctity even at an early age. He became equally known for his learning after his admittance and profession (of religious vows) to the order in the Convent of the Holy Cross in Granada. He became an excellent preacher and was authorized to preach in every region of Spain. He became prior, from 1531 on, of three Dominican Houses concurrently. Though he was never canonized by the Church and was a priest of the highest order from a life of erudition and service, his writings were of the first rank. His works take their place among the classics of Spanish literature. He wrote with the cadences of the poetry of the Bible. Some of his notable treatises: *Prayer and Meditation* (29 editions); *The Guide for Sinners* (18 editions); *The Memorial of the Christian Life* (16 editions); and the mystical *The Introduction to the Symbol of the Faith* (18 editions and numerous versions in Latin, French, and Italian). In its own order, we are told that this work remains unrivaled.[24]

---

24 Sister Felicia, O.S.A., *Seven Spanish Mystics*, Cambridge, Massachusetts, Shea Brothers Press, 1947.

Luis de Granada (1504-1588)
Revelation of the Light of the Holy Cross

Let the sculptors of ages this world emboss

And the waters of knowledge from dams of change

Send a flood to all souls that the saints arrange

By the light and the love of the Holy Cross

In reflection I hang like the Spanish moss

But if skies of Morocco find Atlas strange

I can blend it's cloud-castles and mountain range

Into mystical light of the Holy Cross

In the Cross lies the symbol of three-in-one

Which unravel the sevenfold rainbow keys

And the seven who stand before God aren't done

As they spirit all worlds and the wondrous seas

With the ring of Infinity Godhead spun

Into galaxies sunned by its blazing bees

On the Revelation of the Light of the Holy Cross

In a vision I was shown a luminous cross shrouded in a globular disk of light. The sacred light of the Holy Cross. I was told this is to be the subject of the poem for Luis de Granada, upon whom I was stuck for what to write. There is a spiritual beauty and gift from Divinity in the Light of the Holy Cross. It symbolizes the 1-in-3 and the 3-in-1. This is symbolic of the triplicate expression of the Christian Godhead. Father-Son-Holy Spirit are mirrored in too-numerous-to-name-here ancient, religious traditions, which explain humanity's spiritual relationship to the divine through a triune deity. The disk or ring of light is the ring of Infinity, as also portrayed in the Celtic Christian tradition of the cross with a circle around the intersection. The Almighty created Infinity.

A holy life, and every holy act, is an anchor for Heaven, manifesting the livingness of the holy cross on Earth.

A MYSTIC, TEACHER, AND abbess who totally devoted her energies to her sisters over whom she was in charge and the Order of the Capuchin Poor Clares. Her mystical experience at the age of seven when she was restored from death's door by Mother Serafina, she would later describe: "My childhood ended when I was seven. From then on, I was already a judicious and adroit woman, and therefore patient, measured, silent and truthful." She was accepted in the order at age eleven but had to wait 5 years to take the veil. Another evidence of how intellectually advanced she was. Her deep meditations on the Liturgy of the Hours and other prayer regimens gifted her with a contemplative ministry within the church. She had a life graced with mystical experience, many of which she wrote about.

"I know very well that the Lord does not lead everyone by the same route, and that therefore I have (to) help them, gently and kindly, at the pace which He has decided for each one, without trying to regiment them and direct them all in the same way. My usual way of acting is to do everything under the gaze of my divine Lord. If I suffer, I accept it, exercise patience, and say nothing, I renounce my own pleasure, my will, and way of understanding, I consent to the opinion of others and give way humbly in matters of little consequence. I revere in my sisters that hidden holiness which God has infused in their souls. I accept the way they are, knowing that we are all fragile vessels. I am not surprised by their weaknesses, in fact I suffer with them, because weakness can hinder growth in holiness and in the service of God, and it is an unworthy thing to serve without great holiness, purity and humility. This is why I carry this burden with them." –from the writings of Maria Angela Astorch.[25]

------

25 Blessed Maria Angela Astorch, *Capuchin Franciscan Friars Australia*, ©2021, Web accessed 18 June 2022. https://www.capdox.capuchin.org.au/saints-blesseds/blessed-maria-angela-astorch/

Maria Angela Astorch (1592-1665)

Please go, my love of loves, to heaven and return to me

Give them my askings from my basket of reckless foibles

My human bouquet of acts that wove and destroyed

Don't forget my regret, my hindsight that loses its savor

From experience gained from the lost and the failed

Reap ether and offer my wordless wind to God

The nothingness of my solemn surrender

I've thrown upon altars too high to maintain

Please hail my solar angel and gather rays of radiance

Carry them in boxes locked by hermetic utterance

To block the centaurs of creation who circle

I seek one light of true illumination

Not reflection in pools of my own making

A-thrash in a sensate circus

The façade of a thousand fools

The revelation of sacred rain taps at my window

I receive without giving, I was loved before loving

PETER OF ALCANTARA LIVED a beatific life of ascetic austerity amidst the churn of reform in the Catholic Church in Spain. His fasting and penances to purify and simplify his life were above and beyond the requirements of monastic life. As an example, he wore a coarse hair shirt next to his skin for 20 years. His renown of prophecy, levitation at Holy Mass in religious rapture, and his interactions as if meeting Christ in each person, preceded him. When he first met Teresa of Avila, he told her what contradictions and afflictions she suffered from her ghostly (spiritual confessors) fathers, and other spiritual persons who would…persuade her…that she was seduced (by Satan); and moreover, that she was to suffer much more in the same kind. He likewise foretold what should be the success in the Indies. He often restored sick people in hospitals miraculously to former health.[26]

From aristocratic birth, Peter became a novice in a Franciscan convent when only sixteen years old. Eight years later he was ordained a priest. To this vocation he responded with complete fidelity and self-forgetfulness. His fame (as priest, mystic and spiritual author, and administrator) spread throughout Spain and Portugal. In 1538 he was elected Provincial superior of his province. Here, his real work of reform began to improve his order. He had the graces of contemplation and the most profound penitence. He befriended Teresa of Avila, whom he met in 1558. He became her great advisor and confidante. He spent himself in support of her loyally defending her against detractors and encouraging her to go forward with the new Convent of Saint Joseph. He fasted habitually but taught moderation. Through his *Golden Treatise of Mental Prayer,* he is a living force to this day. It witnesses to the perfect understanding of mystical experience and the ways of mental prayer. … an inexhaustible treasury of spiritual direction for the devout pilgrim on the road to Eternity.[27]

---

26 Alcantara, Peter de, O.S.F., *A Golden Treatise of Mental Prayer,* Willoughby, Giles (translator/biographer), Philadelphia, M. Fithian, 1844.

27 Sister Felicia, O.S.A., *Seven Spanish Mystics,* Cambridge, Massachusetts, Shea Brothers Press, 1947.

Peter of Alcantara (1499-1562)

I often hear songs of a vibrant sky lark
This joy from the world knows I'll reach the high peaks
To navigate vision divinity speaks
Where light will fall piercing the dens in the dark

To nourish the earth with the truth in a myth
I carry a sack of its seeds with great care
Like rings of the doves as they coil through the air
To sow round the hills my glad highway therewith

We met on dark streets; I hold riddles and keys
Despite the dank cities that flicker through haze
You asked for an apple; by moonlight you'll graze
Where cinnamon grows with the cloves and a breeze

In halls of devotion I found a lit path
Where priests have thrice-blessed my small prayer that has flown
The skyway to nothingness, spirit alone
For eagles aren't prey to the desert's blind wrath

I stand in the doorway, a castle uphill
Where people come carting life's load in the heart
To press the tight gate or to make a new start
Yet find the best entry by wisdom and will

THROUGH A COMPLEX HISTORY of political families vying for the throne, Constanza of Castilla, of royal lineage, became a nun and eventual prioress of one of the largest Dominican Convents in Spain, Santo Domingo El Real in Madrid. She authored a prayer book, *Devotio y oficio* and composed most of its prayers. A nurturer of unusual spirituality derived from prioress responsibilities, she was maternal, contemplative, and teacher. Her royal family connections as cousin to the queen surrounded her with strong female role models, who supported one another. Constanza influenced the lives of nuns in her convent, educating them within those walls. Her *Oracion* was an extended meditation on the life of Jesus. Through her teaching on the *compassio* or compassion of Mary, she gave her nuns a way to remain feminine in their spirituality.[28]

---

28 Surtz, Ronald, *Writing Women in Late Medieval and Early Modern Spain: The Mothers of Saint Teresa of Avila*, Philadelphia, University of Pennsylvania Press, 1995.

Constanza de Castilla (1395-1478)

Compassion's song, your citadel

From inside out old trappings fell

You raised a chapel for a king

And built a house where church bells swing

A prioress' princess cell

Through Mary's window I could tell

My prayers with her became a well

So deep with love that I could sing

Compassion's song

For in my princedom nuns would swell

And contemplation came to dwell

In hearts and minds that drank its spring

My litanies to Mary bring

Alignment so that hearts compel

Compassion's song

Francisco de Osuna wrote six ascetic and mystical works called *Spiritual Alphabets.* These works were another influencer of Teresa of Avila, introducing to her at a young age the concept of the Prayer of Quiet. It is considered a masterpiece of Franciscan Mysticism. His premise in the book is that friendship and communion with God are possible in this life through cleansing one's conscience, entering one's heart, resting in loving stillness, and then rising above the heart to God alone.

De Osuna's six subjects of the *Spiritual Alphabets* in general are the Passion, asceticism, contemplation, love, poverty, and the wounds of Jesus.[29]

---

29 Egan, Harvey D., S.J., *An Anthology of Christian Mysticism,* Collegeville, The Liturgical Press, 1991.

Francisco de Osuna (1497-1541)

A part of God, I sail a path

Blue-gray, then ocean all a-shimmer

Can icy ages show a glimmer?

Discovered ancients close to me

Each day they blog the human tree

Forensic studies shine, yet dimmer

Apart from God

Blue Nile outlasts Goliath of Gath

Can cataracts find one brave swimmer?

Discover stars that seethe and simmer

Each lunge for light is holy math

For a part in God

ISABEL WAS BORN IN Guadalajara, Spain of "*conversos*" (Jewish converts) descent and a seamstress profession. As a child she had some mystical experiences. She left home early (returning after some years) to develop her spirituality and later became a *beata* as a Tertiary Franciscan. One of the original and most influential women theologians of the first three decades of the 16th century, she led a progressive group, termed the *Alumbrados* by Spanish authorities, or The Enlightened/The Illuminists. The roots were in Gnosticism. The followers of Sister Isabel de la Cruz believed that through inner purification their souls should submit to God's will and thus bridge direct communication with God. Her concept of *dejamiento* (meditative abandonment) utilized a form of mental prayer, an abandonment to God, different from the orthodox *recogimiento* (recollection or gathering), which used vocal prayer. *Dejamiento*, she taught, led to immersion in God. Conversely, she taught that certain Church teachings were unnecessary.

While they counted some of the high aristocracy among their number, this movement was crushed and terminated by the Spanish Inquisition and most records of imprisonment/banishment were secreted away.[30]

---

30 Longhurst, John E., *La Beata Isabel de la Cruz ante la Inquisicion*, 1524-1529, Cuadernos de Historia de Espana, 1957.

Isabel de la Cruz (late 15th to mid-16ᵗʰ c.)

The star plateaus are silvered lights

Of Those Who levitate, dreaming like me

Celestial sanctum hides a new moon

Whose someday adorns a planet and night

The Cosmos bends the plumes of novae

Crescendos of symphonies eons ago

The swooping vultures arch in my eyes

The rain fills my lake of translucent yearning

Omniscient owls glide silence to me

The sky gives the blessing that I receive

My hut will not sparkle like pinnacle-spires

Controlling The Way to let gargoyles glisten

A Priest Forever, after the Order of Melchizedek

The title of this painting is taken from the scripture verse in Psalm 110:4 and repeated in Hebrews 5:6. The first revelation of the vision of this image was that all souls are called to the royal priesthood, i.e., the path of holiness to God. The second revelation is twofold and lies in the symbolism. The evenly balanced cross symbolizes the path of self-sacrifice for Christians. It also depicts the dual aspects of God. An evenly balanced cosmos of the Father, the divine masculine aspect in the vertical from base to zenith, initiates power and will into the plane of matter, the Mother, the divine feminine aspect of the horizontal breadth nourishing all in manifestation. The golden circle is the plane circumscribing divinity in the physical cosmos (as noted in *The Secret Doctrine*, by Helena Blavatsky). The four red squares are the four elements: Earth, Air, Fire, and Water, encased in the fifth element of Ether (the sea of yellow).

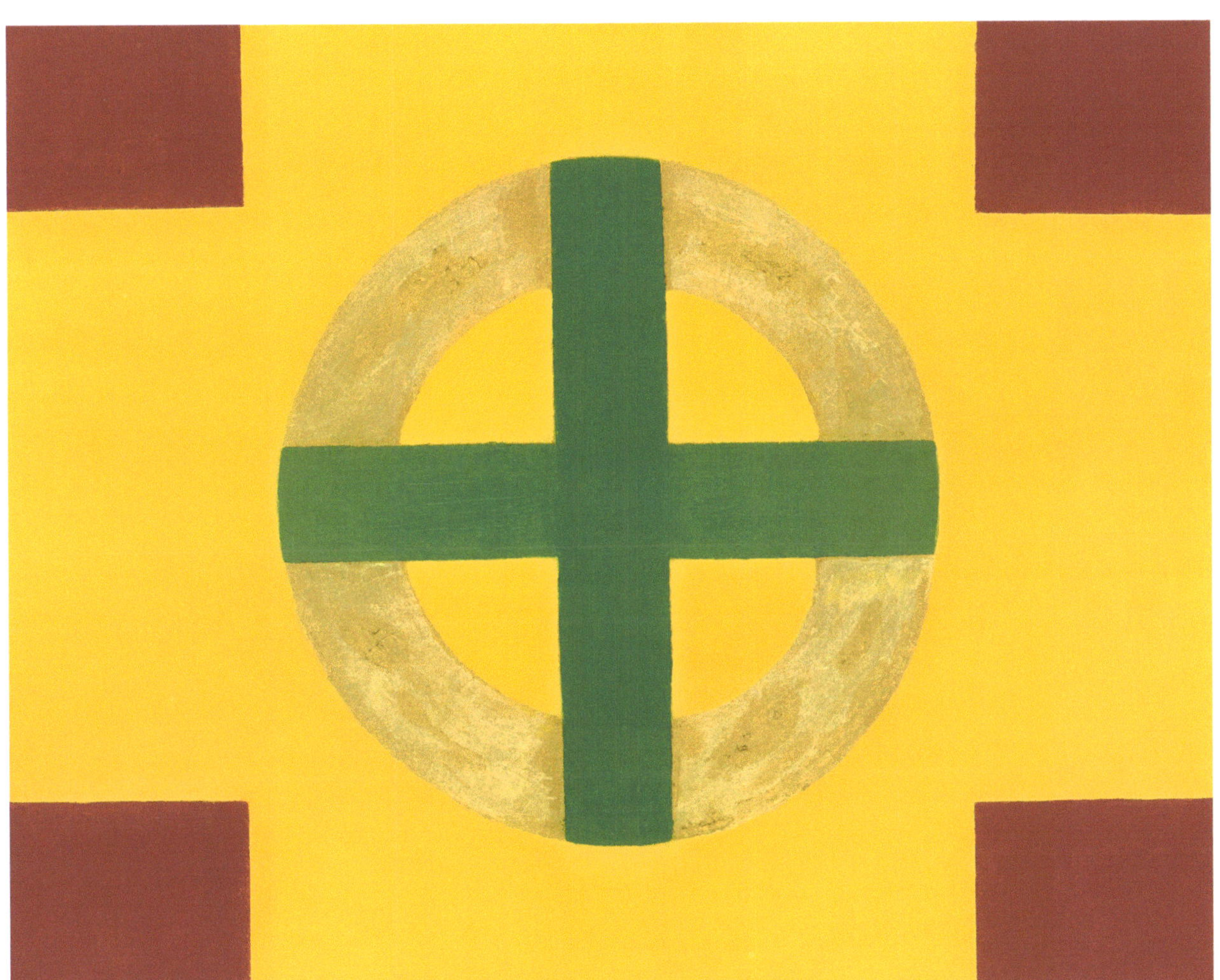

Saint Ignatius, along with Francis Xavier and Peter Faber, founded the Society of Jesus, aka the Jesuit Order. Born to minor Basque nobility. His adolescent heroes were El Cid, knights of Camelot, and other chivalrous tales. Served as a soldier before the priesthood. While recovering from a grave injury to his leg in battle, he discerned a call to religious life through prayer and supernatural experiences and visions. He lived an ascetic life for some time after visiting the monastery of Santa Maria de Montserrat and the town of Manresa. During this time, he was influenced by other teachers and incorporated a type of simple contemplation of placing oneself in a biblical scene during meditation. This became foundational to his book of *Spiritual Exercises.* "… consider how God dwells in the creatures and in the elements, giving them being; in the animals, giving them feeling; in (humanity), giving … understanding…and likewise making a temple of me, since I am created in the similitude and image of His Divine Majesty."[31]

Commonly known as the four elements of creation, Earth, Air, Fire, and Water pertain to the life of the physical world. This quad of energies is known in esoteric circles as the domain of the lower world. That lower world of energy then corresponds to the lower forces of nature in a human being. These are the dominant forces in one's life until the higher nature of the soul with its virtues, assumes control by directing and applying a person's spiritual energy wisely. The effects of a mature religion.

---

31 Thompson, Francis, *Saint Ignatius of Loyola*, Dublin, Burns Oates, 1951.

Ignatius of Loyola (1491-1556), an Espinela

At the dawn it was said of God

And of Heaven, that Love's descent

Is an arc from a bucket bent

On the flooding of worlds abroad

In the physical world, our quad

Is the twirl of four elements

Yet they thrive by intelligence

And together emit their ray

Via choirs that sing each day

In the union of elegance

JUAN DE LOS ANGELES studied at the University of Alcalá, joined the Franciscan Order in the Friars Minor, and spent most of his professional life at the Province of San José (Madrid) preaching, confessing, writing, and traveling on foot in Spain and abroad. He was spiritual director to the Infanta, Sor Margarita de la Cruz (a nun) and preacher to the royal chapter of her mother, the Empress Maria. He remained active, despite illness in later years, until his death.[32] His writings may be seen as a psychological perspective of the mystical; they deal with such problems as the absorption of the soul in God, active and passive recollection, kinds of ecstasy, mystical phenomena, and spiritual enslavement to Mary. His works are numerous. In his words, "…and that little I write like a dwarf on the shoulders of a giant…"[33]

---

32 Peers, E. Allison, *The Mystics of Spain*, London, George Allen & Unwin Ltd., 1951.

33 Peers, E. Allison, *Studies of the Spanish Mystics*, London, Sheldon Press, Vol.1, 1927.

Juan de los Angeles (1536-1609)

With a candle I melted the wax from the bees

From the scriptures I wrote not a paper to please

But to teach with the simplest of words for blest food

To be eaten like honey and drunk 'til imbued

In the radiant light, this is life, not a frieze

In the depths of a dungeon there's fruit on the trees

Once the jailer has left and has taken the keys

And bereft of distractions, the darkness I chewed

With a candle

There's a climb up a mountain, a swim across seas

At the ridge there is rest for the body to ease

Where exertion finds union as mind is subdued

And a vanishing sunset lets silence intrude

With a candle

As a baby, Juana displayed extraordinary religious experiences. She made her mind up as a child to become a nun. At the age of 15 she entered the convent at Santa Maria de la Cruz in Cubas, Spain. As a nun, she practiced a harsh ascetism which upset other nuns in the convent. She continued to experience mystical raptures. Juana became abbess in 1509. She pronounced sermons (locutions) in her mystical trances which drew attention and attendance from important personages. She was falsely betrayed by one of her nuns and was removed for several years from her leadership position, until a full confession of the false accusation obtained from the accusing nun on her deathbed restored Juana's role as abbess.[34]

[Abattoirs: slaughterhouses

Cygnus: The constellation in the celestial northern hemisphere depicting a great swan, entailing the astronomical asterism of the Northern Cross.]

---

34 Surtz, Ronald, *Writing Women in Late Medieval and Early Modern Spain: The Mothers of Saint Teresa of Avila*, Philadelphia, University of Pennsylvania Press, 1995.

Juana de la Cruz (1481-1534)

The mystic children plant and farm by distant light
They till a field no longer for the czars
They paint a subtle world in barn-red bright

It wasn't love that cost the Spaniards epic blight
The convent wasn't refuge from the wars
The mystic children plant and farm by distant light

With humble springs I wash my eyes for second sight
A tattered coat I wear to hide my scars
Then paint the subtle worlds so barn-red bright

They polished oaken chests of truth in black and white
Some butchers used it for their abattoirs
The mystic children plant and farm by distant light

The eagle's life means death to those who feel its might
I died to life's flamenco with guitars
I'll paint a subtle world in barn-red bright

The swan supreme, O Cygnus, flies the sky of night
The Northern Cross, my path to all the stars
The mystic children plant and farm by distant light
They paint a subtle world in barn-red bright

Garcia de Cisneros was an Abbot of Montserrat (Santa Maria de Montserrat Abbey on the mountain of the same name in Catalonia, Spain). He authored the *Book of Exercises for the Spiritual Life*, (and) had gone to that famous house from the Benedictine monastery at Valladolid to reform it, and the Book of Exercises was written for his own monks, in order to lay firm spiritual foundations on which his reforms were to be built. The goal it envisages is the goal of the mystic, 'the uniting of the soul with God'. This book was widely published internationally in its day and into the modern centuries recognized and used. It heavily influenced religious life and those who later influenced reform including, among others, Saint Ignatius of Loyola.[35]

---

35 Peers, E. Allison, *The Mystics of Spain*, London, George Allen & Unwin Ltd., 1951.

GARCIA DE CISNEROS (1455-1510)

Across the Catalan lands, a mount renown
Once called a priest, the one who came to crown
The heart, whose light devotion stokes to flame
Removing smoke that smears the mortared walls
To clear the inner paths in lanterned halls

A monastery has two doors of gold
An abbot or an abbess serves the fold
Of hearts, whose light devotion stokes to flame
One portal serves the human world of things
The other parts two worlds and inward swings

A rule of rhythm trains the soul in flesh
As incense blends the oak and stone to mesh
With hearts, whose light devotion stokes to flame
As silence towers over any yoke
With gifts of revelation, monks awoke

For cadence of my life I whittled wood
The soul, it has a goal, for love makes good
The heart, whose light devotion stokes to flame
The darkest roads that knew my name were old
They led me to the country love foretold

The Holiness of Creation

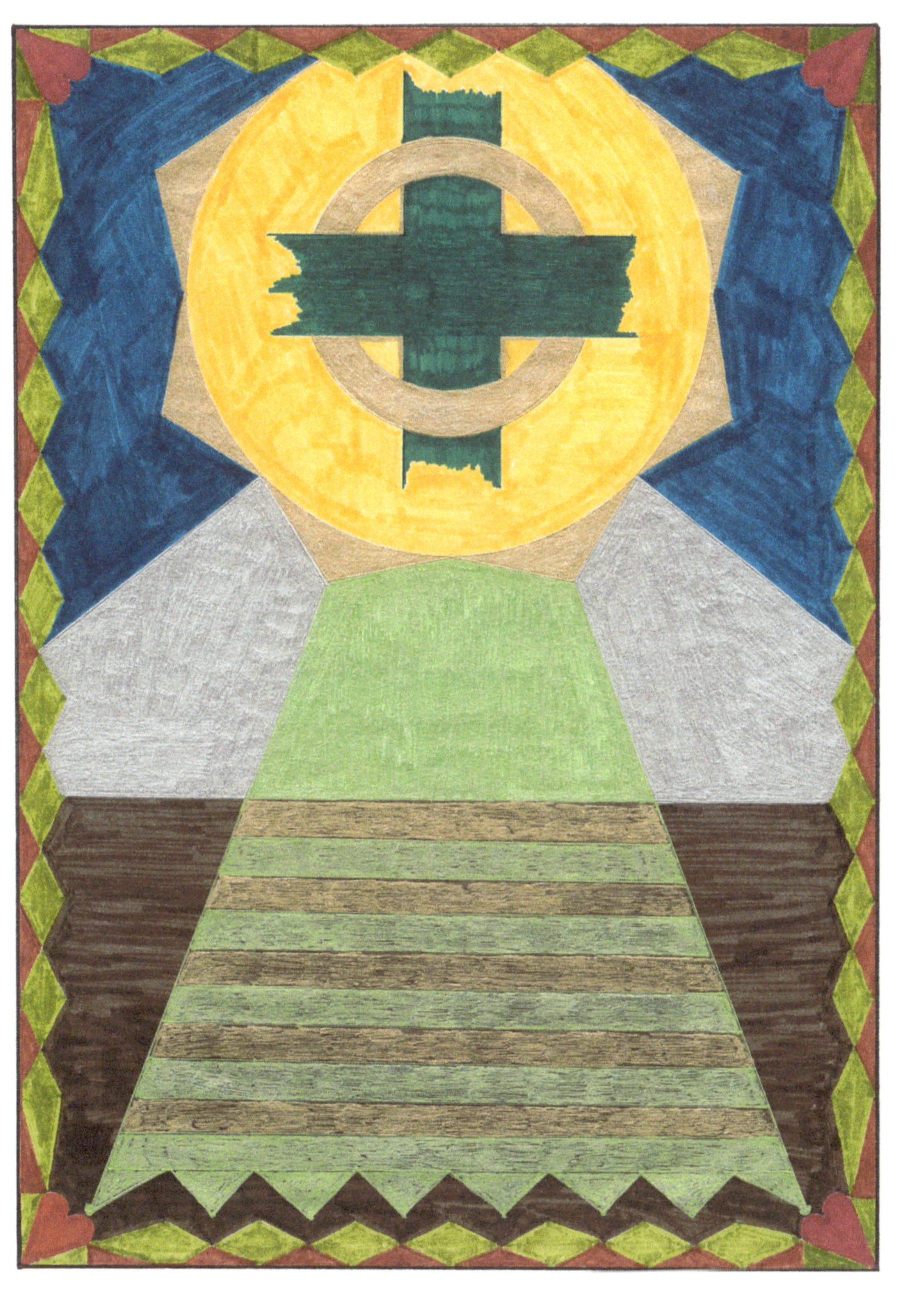

Known as "The Beata of Piedrahita", Maria was born to lowly farmers. Maria at an early age was drawn to prayer. She became a *beata* first and took the habit of the Third Order of Saint Dominic at the monastery of Santo Domingo in Piedrahita at the age of sixteen. As a beata, she chose to live by the rules of the Dominican Order, but without taking formal vows of a nun. Her ecstasies and revelations eventually brought her to the court of King Ferdinand, and audiences with the Duke of Alba, Cardinal Cisneros and later, the Spanish Inquisition. At one point she was ordered to assess and help reform the Dominican monastery in Toledo. Accruing opposition from this daunting task, her accusers tried to defame her. After four investigations, she was cleared from her interviews with the Inquisition by virtue of her exemplary life and the support of her highly positioned political comrades. Later, she was set up with a prioress position at her own convent in Piedrahita.[36]

---

36 Surtz, Ronald, *Writing Women in Late Medieval and Early Modern Spain: The Mothers of Saint Teresa of Avila*, Philadelphia, University of Pennsylvania Press, 1995.

Maria de Santo Domingo (1486-1524)

Once a girl in a farmhouse constrained a wild stream
As it flowed from a city, divinity's truth
From the dark come the words that fulfill a new dream
Like a gale to a sail, or like love in your youth

It is known by the Spirit, its path we must choose
And each person can follow a road, high or low
Even roads into darkness will post us the clues
With a gift there's a calling where one ought to go

I will drink from the stream my Beloved will flow
I will shake every tree for the fruit of my muse
Under moon, under sun, under Milky Way's glow
I will wonder the Ancient of Days in these pews

And when nothing appears in my eyes but the light
From the portal that opens to freedom they'll say
El Camino was mapped from the heaven-lit height
And each soul to the dance of celestial ballet

Antonio Margil de Jesus was born in Valencia, Spain, on August 18, 1657. As a young boy, Margil expressed his desire to become a Franciscan. On April 22, 1673, he received the order's habit at La Corona de Cristo in Valencia. Then at the age of twenty-five, he received Holy Orders and soon accepted the challenge of missionary work in New Spain. He also spent time as a missionary in Yucatán, Costa Rica, and Guatemala. After a brief illness in early 1716, he traveled to East Texas to set up Franciscan missions. When he arrived in July, Margil supervised the founding of Nuestra Señora de Los Dolores and San Miguel de Los Adaes. Then in February of 1720, he founded at San Antonio, the most successful of all Texas missions, San José y San Miguel de Aguayo. Even though his career in Texas was short, he is one of the most famous missionaries to serve in Texas.

In 1717 a terrible drought in Nacogdoches caused the springs to dry out. Then, one day, Father Margil de Jesus went out to the banks of Lanana Creek. He carried with him images of saints and his staff. With his staff, he struck a rock and immediately fresh water flowed through the creek. Some consider Father Margil to be a second Moses with his Nacogdoches miracle.[37]

[Southern Cross: a bright and recognizable constellation in the Southern Hemisphere]

---

37 Emily Smith, "Fray Antonio Margil de Jesus (1657–1726)," *East Texas History*, accessed August 2, 2022, https://easttexashistory.org/items/show/315

Antonio Margil de Jesus (1657-1726)

The Living Brevity

For foreign lands I would fly like a loon

As sea creatures migrate the gray and the blue

But guarding my hut that hugs a white dune

Prismatic birds are imprisoned in hue

As a jaguar, high in trees that are true

I hopped into chasms of Indian eyes

On pyramids kings let ocelots rise

The Southern Cross of the stars called to me

A nomad of shifting clouds in disguise

Of the living brevity all can be

WRITING WAS USUALLY THE duty of the clergy who were male. Teresa, a nun, was an exception. With a disease of gradual deafness over time, Teresa spent a large part of her life in the convent of Salamanca or Burgos. In her writings, specifically the *Arboleta*, Teresa considered the suffering of illness a blessing because it taught the virtue of patience. In turn, this would lead to spiritual health and salvation. In her treatise *Admiracion,* she claims the biblical Judith as her spiritual mother, and defends writing her treatise (as a woman author) based on parallels with the non-customary (for her gender in the Middle Ages) triumph of Judith wielding a sword to defeat the people's enemy, Holofernes. Later she writes about the miracle of Jesus and the blind man. In identifying with these two biblical characters of Judith and the blind man, '...the roles... turn out to be emblems of her splendid isolation'.

In her forced meditative world of deafness and the isolation it brought, Teresa found great blessing in the spiritual exercise of religious writings to communicate her revelations of God.[38]

[For context, the average lay person and certainly peasants in the Middle Ages were illiterate. The primary avenue of education was through the monastic system and the Church.]

---

38 Surtz, Ronald, *Writing Women in Late Medieval and Early Modern Spain: The Mothers of Saint Teresa of Avila*, Philadelphia, University of Pennsylvania Press, 1995.

TERESA DE CARTAGENA (1425-?)

From your island of silence the boats retreat

As you scale every hill until clouds you meet

Where you feel the warm touch of the soul's caress

With as much you can stay until dawn you greet

As the Spirit makes known the beloved you bless

When the church was my guide and a rook of steel

Where I buried all sorrows that one can feel

There I found a new mother to whom I confess

And her purest of priests was the prince of zeal

For the Spirit makes known the beloved you bless

And within is a mansion whose stairway goes

To the rooms which need keys the beholder stows

And through seven oak doors must the mind address

What the heart truly wants from the peace that flows

From the Spirit Who knows the beloved you bless

Revelations float ships that will rise with the rain

I am out on its ocean and wide-eyed sane

With a heart that is open, for nothing less

Lets us master the waters that still remain

Where the Spirit makes known the beloved you bless

Converted, as a young man, from a life of ease and dissipation, Lull (also Llull) devoted fifty years of a long life to missionary work… in particular among the Moors. He was a voluminous writer, authoring 250 (or more) works. In his *Book of the Lover and Beloved*, he wrote: "…certain men called Sufis set down words of love and brief examples which give men great devotion…thereof the understanding soars aloft, and the will likewise soars, and is increased in devotion." He was martyred in North Africa, and two centuries were to pass before Spain—a newly united country (in the early 1500's)—could produce a mystic of comparable stature.[39]

---

39 Peers, E. Allison, *The Mystics of Spain*, London, George Allen & Unwin Ltd., 1951.

Ramon Lull (1233-1315)

On the ark of Majorca eloping with song of his life

In the silence of moonlight's asylum of love, in a blink

Rose the notes of sweet lyrics beloved to man, as a wife

Whom he loved, as she wept for pure love from a mountain's high brink

In the age of ideals came the Christians from Palestine's shore

And then Islam prepared a new banquet as bride from the East

From the kingdom of Jews, the first daughter, the times would deplore

With philosophy I shall then call all the righteous to feast

O, the germ of the wheat of my words comes by grinding a mill

And indulges the virtue of law from a God disappeared

If not glory, then what is the grist that the world offers still?

From my palace of ice, I from sea to the sky, commandeered

And I gaze into light as a thief for Eternity's gold

Where I contemplate spiraling orbs in a billion-starred-sea

Where the whitecaps of Cosmos will die on the banks of its hold

That collects every sight of my thought, as it contemplates me

AS A YOUNG MAN in Spain, Didacus lived for some time as a hermit. He became a Franciscan brother and developed a reputation for great insight into God's ways. His penances were heroic. He was so generous with the poor that the friars sometimes grew uneasy about his charity. Didacus volunteered for the missions in the Canary Islands and was the superior of a friary there. In 1450 he attended the canonization of Saint Bernardine of Siena. When many of the friars gathered for that celebration fell ill, Didacus stayed in Rome for three months to nurse them. (Author's note: Miracles of healing followed his pious prayers). After he returned to Spain, he pursued a life of contemplation full-time. He showed the friars the wisdom of God's ways.[40]

[Diego was also known as Didacus (Latin), San Diego de Alcala, and San Diego de San Nicolas del Puerto. The city of San Diego, California bears his name.]

---

40 Habig, Marion, *The Franciscan Book of Saints*, Chicago, Franciscan Herald Press, 1979.

Diego of Alcala (c.1400-1463), an Espinela

Diego of Alcala lies

Asleep beneath the centuries

Alive in deeds like ancient trees

Whose wisdom blossoms in demise

Invisibly the ego dies

In simple life within my prime

As hermit's ways will master Time

When days of contemplation tell

And nights of revelation spell

Great mysteries that ever mime

Author's Note

Ronnie Smith grew up in Chicago, Illinois and Baltimore, Maryland. He earned a bachelor's degree at Loyola University Maryland, and later studied engineering at the University of Maryland. Colonel Smith, retired from the Air Force after 30 years of service, where he commanded or flew over 1,000 flights in Antarctica as well as serving in Air Force/U.N. missions on all the other continents. Challenged by extreme winds and temperatures that could drop to minus 75 degrees Fahrenheit during Antarctic summer, physical and mental endurance were paramount to combat the rigors of prolonged operational stress. He discovered in that world contemplation and divine majesty. His poetry and paintings rest upon the foundation of the underlying wonder of God in humanity and creation. He hopes to develop a spiritual retreat center to allow participants to reconnect to their own God-centered inner world, experienced in a sanctuary of the divine natural world.

If you have enjoyed reading this book, please post a review, long or short, on any book distributor sites (Amazon, Barnes and Noble, etc.). It is very appreciated and helps promote the work.

If you would like to place a bulk order for your parish, school, or friends, then please note that we offer special discounts on quantity purchases made by corporations, associations, schools, and others. For details or any comments, contact the author at:

Ronnie Smith/Plenus Gratia Publications

PlenusGratiaToday@gmail.com

www.PlenusGratia.com

9 781735 659541